FROM SEA to SHINING SEA

NEW MEXICO

THERESE DE ANGELIS

Consultants

MELISSA N. MATUSEVICH, PH.D.

Curriculum and Instruction Specialist
Blacksburg, Virginia

KATE HARRINGTON, LIBRARIAN

Albuquerque/Bernalillo County Library System
Albuquerque, New Mexico

ALISON E. ALMQUIST, M.L.S., M.A.

Wherry Elementary School
Albuquerque, New Mexico

P30⁵⁰

CHILDREN'S PRESS®

A DIVISION OF SCHOLASTIC INC.

New York • Toronto • London • Auckland • Sydney • Mexico City
New Delhi • Hong Kong • Danbury, Connecticut

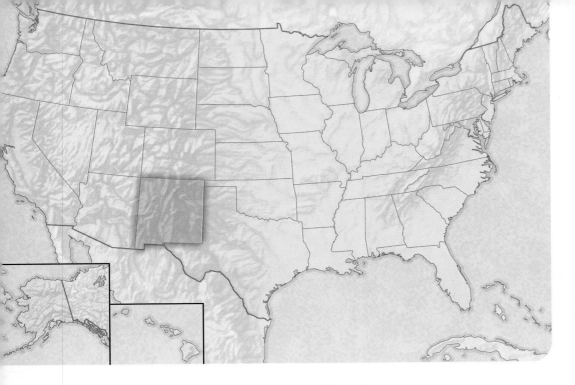

New Mexico is in the southwestern part of the United States. It is bordered by Colorado, Arizona, Texas, Oklahoma, Utah, and Mexico.

The front cover photo shows young boys selling local products at a gift shop in Taos.

Project Editor: Meredith DeSousa
Art Director: Marie O'Neill
Photo Researcher: Marybeth Kavanagh
Design: Robin West, Ox and Company, Inc.
Page 6 map and recipe art: Susan Hunt Yule
All other maps: XNR Productions, Inc.

Library of Congress Cataloging-in-Publication Data

De Angelis, Therese.
    New Mexico / by Therese De Angelis.
      p. cm. -- (From sea to shining sea)
    ISBN 0-516-22381-X
      1. New Mexico--Juvenile literature. [1. New Mexico.] I. Title.
II. From sea to shining sea (Series)

F796.3 .D4 2002
978.9--dc21   2001006984

TABLE of CONTENTS

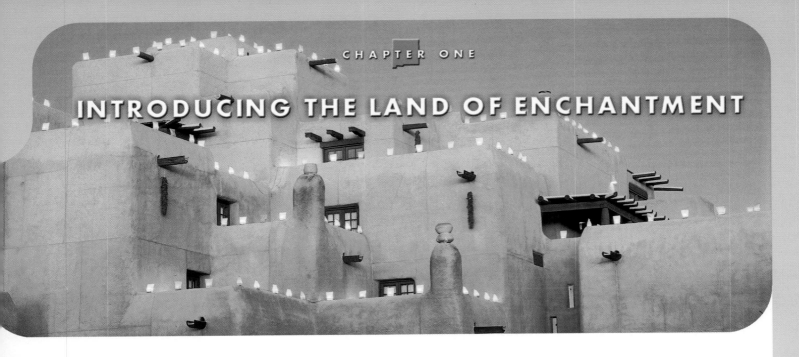

CHAPTER ONE

INTRODUCING THE LAND OF ENCHANTMENT

The adobe-style architecture in New Mexico today echoes the adobe creations of the state's early Native Americans.

New Mexico is so big that you could fit Connecticut, Delaware, Washington, D.C., New Jersey, New York, Pennsylvania, and Rhode Island into it and still have plenty of room left over! New Mexico is the fifth largest state in the country. It stretches 121,598 square miles (314,937 square kilometers) in an almost rectangular shape. A small "boot heel" at the southwestern corner of the state juts into Mexico, a country to the south of New Mexico.

East of New Mexico are Oklahoma and Texas. To the south are Texas and the country of Mexico. To the west is Arizona, and to the north is Colorado. New Mexico's northwest boundary lines crisscross with those of Arizona, Colorado, and Utah to form a place called the Four Corners—the only place in the United States where four states meet.

New Mexico has been a state for less than one hundred years. In 1610, the area that is now New Mexico was claimed by Spain. In 1821 it became part of Mexico. Later, New Mexico became a United States territory, but it did not become a state until 1912.

Almost all of New Mexico is higher than 4,000 feet (1,220 meters) above sea level. Even though the powerful Rio Grande runs through the state, New Mexico has very little water, and much of the land is desert. The state also contains thick forests, towering mountain peaks, grassy plains, plateaus, valleys, cliffs, and canyons. In fact, New Mexico's beautiful landscapes and wildlife give it the nickname "the Land of Enchantment."

What comes to mind when you think of New Mexico?

- Ancient Native Americans living in pueblos carved out of rocky cliffs
- Spanish explorers establishing settlements four hundred years ago
- Birds taking refuge at Bosque del Apache National Wildlife Refuge
- Cowboys driving cattle along the Santa Fe Trail
- People claiming to have seen a UFO near Roswell
- Tourists exploring abandoned "ghost towns" of the Old West
- Roadrunners feeding on lizards and snakes
- Hispanics celebrating their heritage with the music, song, and dance of Mexico

New Mexico means all of these things and many more. Welcome to the Land of Enchantment!

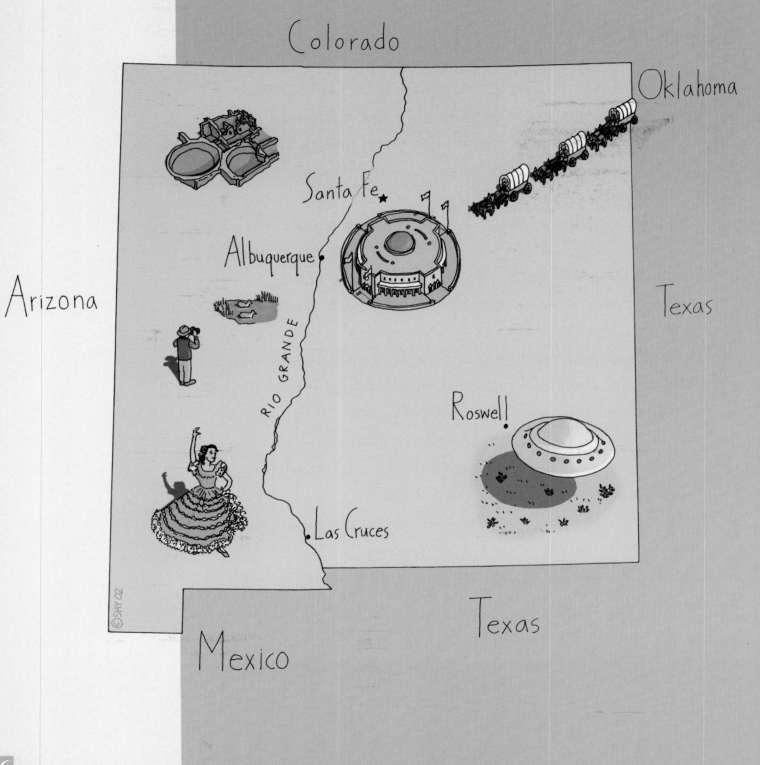

Colorado

Oklahoma

Arizona

Texas

Santa Fe ★

Albuquerque •

RIO GRANDE

Roswell •

Las Cruces •

Texas

Mexico

©SHY 02

6

CHAPTER TWO

THE LAND OF NEW MEXICO

New Mexico is full of natural wonders, from mountains and canyons to high-topped plateaus and mesas. The land of New Mexico is divided into four geographic regions: the Great Plains (east), the Rocky Mountains (north central), the Colorado Plateau (northwest), and the Basin and Range (southwest and central).

Many visitors come to New Mexico to enjoy its scenic beauty.

THE GREAT PLAINS

Most of eastern New Mexico is part of a semi-arid region called the Great Plains. Semi-arid regions get small amounts of rainfall, between 10 and 20 inches (25 and 51 centimeters) per year. Buffalo grasses and blue grama—the official state grass—grow in the Great Plains region. Pronghorns (antelope-like animals) and cattle graze there.

Most cities in this area, such as Raton, Cimarron, Springer, Las Vegas, and Tucumcari, were founded centuries ago. The region's best-known city is Roswell, the fourth-largest city in New Mexico. Others include Clovis, Artesia, Hobbs, and Carlsbad.

The Canadian and Pecos Rivers run through the Great Plains region. East of the Pecos is an area called Llano Estacado, which lies in northeast New Mexico and part of Texas. Some people say that the name, which means "staked plains," describes the way the tall yucca plants rise like a series of stakes across the flat landscape. This region was described by early explorer Francisco Vásquez de Coronado as "plains so vast, that I did not find their limit anywhere I went. . ."

UTAH

COLORADO

KANS.

OKLAHOMA

San Juan River

Farmington

▲ Shiprock

COLORADO
PLATEAU

ROCKY MTS.

Wheeler Peak
13,161 ft./
4,011 m ▲

SANGRE DE CRISTO MTS.

Chama River

Abiquiu
Reservoir

ARIZONA

Santa Fe ✪

Conchas
Lake

Canadian River

Albuquerque

Rio Grande

Sumner
Lake

Pecos River

TEXAS

Elephant
Butte
Reservoir

SACRAMENTO MTS.

G R E A T

Bottomless
Lakes

P L A I N S

Gila River

BASIN
AND RANGE

Hobbs

N

MEXICO

0   40   80 mi.

0   40   80 km

13,124 ft.	4,000 m
6,562 ft.	2,000 m
4,921 ft.	1,500 m
3,281 ft.	1,000 m
1,640 ft.	500 m
820 ft.	250 m
0	0

THE ROCKY MOUNTAINS

The north central region of New Mexico is at the southern end of the Rocky Mountains. The Rocky Mountains extend all the way from central New Mexico to Alaska. Sometimes called the Rockies, this mountain range roughly follows what is called the Continental Divide, or the Great Divide. This is the geographical line that divides rivers flowing to different sides of the continent. Rivers west of the Rockies flow toward the Pacific Ocean, while rivers east of the range flow toward the Atlantic Ocean.

East of the Rio Grande are the Sangre de Cristo Mountains. Many of New Mexico's tallest peaks are there. Wheeler Peak is the highest point in New Mexico at 13,161 feet (4,011 m). It is more than 2 miles (3.2 km) high. West of the Rio Grande are the Jemez and Nacimiento Mountains. The largest cities in this region are Santa Fe, Los Alamos, and Taos.

THE COLORADO PLATEAU

West of the Rocky Mountains is the Colorado Plateau. There, a broad desert valley surrounds the San Juan River as it flows westward. Below the Navajo Dam, the valley becomes green and fertile. Cliffs, canyons, mesas (high, steep rock formations with flat tops), and arroyos (the beds of creeks or small streams that are usually dry) break up much of the Colorado Plateau region.

Thousands of years ago, this area contained many active volcanoes. The strange volcanic formations led early Spanish explorers to name the area El Malpais, "the badlands." The largest cities and towns of the Colorado Plateau are Farmington, Gallup, and Grants.

The Bisti Badlands, located in the northwestern corner of New Mexico, contain unusual rock formations and eroded clay mounds.

THE BASIN AND RANGE REGION

The Basin and Range region covers one-third of southern and central New Mexico. It is made up of low, wide deserts and fertile valleys and farmlands (or ranges) along the Rio Grande. The region is also dotted with mountains, including the Black, Florida (pronounced "Flor-EYE-da"), Magdalena, Sandia, and San Mateo Mountains.

The largest city in this region is Albuquerque. Another large city, Silver City, was founded in the 1800s when settlers and miners arrived to mine for gold, silver, and copper. Many frontier towns became retreats for notorious outlaws.

The Gila National Forest is located in the Basin and Range region. It is one of the largest national forests in the United States, covering

3.3 million acres (1.3 million hectares). This wilderness area has some of the most spectacular mountain views in the Southwest.

Outside the Sacramento Mountains is a dazzling snow-white desert that spans 144,000 acres (58,277 ha). This is the White Sands National Monument. The "sand" is actually glistening crystals of a mineral called gypsum. Rain

The landscape of White Sands National Monument is constantly changing.

washes the gypsum down from nearby mountains, and dry winds carry it to the basin and crush it to sandlike bits. The gypsum forms sparkling dunes up to 60 feet (18 m) high.

Near Alamogordo, at a place called Trinity Site, lies a crater—a huge, bowl-shaped hole in the ground. It was formed when scientists exploded the world's first atomic bomb, a powerful, deadly weapon, on July 16, 1945. Nearby is Las Cruces, the state's second-largest city. The southern Rio Grande region is also New Mexico's richest agricultural area.

The state's longest and most important river is the Rio Grande.

RIVERS AND LAKES

New Mexico is one of the driest states because it receives very little rainfall. The state's biggest source of water is the Rio Grande, which flows for 1,800 miles (2,896 km) from the mountains of Colorado to the Gulf of Mexico. Three rivers flow into the Rio Grande in New Mexico: the Jemez, the Chama, and the Red Rivers. Other major rivers are the Canadian, Pecos, Gila, and San Juan Rivers.

Because water is so scarce in New Mexico, especially in the

south, a system of human-made channels brings water to the places it is most needed. This system of channels, sometimes called acequias, is used for irrigation. The Pecos and San Juan Rivers provide water that is used for irrigation. The United States Bureau of Reclamation manages dams at Carlsbad, Fort Sumner, and Tucumcari to increase water supplies for the state. Other irrigation projects have been built in the Colorado River basin. Elephant Butte Reservoir on the Rio Grande is a major source of irrigation for New Mexico's farmlands. The water problem is so severe in New Mexico that, in 1998, Governor Gary Johnson announced the creation of a statewide "Drought Plan." The plan helps local, state, and federal organizations work with businesses and residents to prevent major problems during extremely dry years.

Elephant Butte Reservoir provides water for the state's farmland.

The Bottomless Lakes near Roswell are the most famous natural lakes in New Mexico. The bluish-green color of the water in these eight lakes (seven of which are in Bottomless Lakes State Park) makes them look bottomless, but the deepest lake is only 90 feet (27 m) deep. Most of New

Mexico's lakes are human-made, or artificial. They were created to help irrigate the land. The largest artificial lakes are Elephant Butte Reservoir and Conchas Reservoir.

CLIMATE

New Mexico has the greatest range in regional temperatures of any state in America. The weather is usually warm and dry, with sunshine and low humidity, which is the degree of moisture or dampness in the air. Summer temperatures sizzle at 90° Fahrenheit (32° Celsius) during the day and cool to 50°F (10°C) at night. Winter temperatures range from about 35°F (2°C) in the north to 55°F (13°C) in the south. Heat waves, prolonged periods of very high temperatures (usually over 100°F/38°C) sometimes occur in southern areas of New Mexico.

Most of New Mexico receives little precipitation (rain, snow, and hail). The average annual precipitation is 13 inches (33 cm). Droughts, long periods of dry weather in which little or no precipitation falls, are fairly common in New Mexico.

Because the state is so dry, most farmers cannot simply wait for rainfall. Instead, more than half the farms in New Mexico are irrigated. The only region that receives heavy precipitation is the northern mountain ranges. As much as 300 inches (762 cm) of snow may fall there in winter.

This drawing shows a typical morning in Santa Fe Plaza in the 1800s.

Scientists believe that the first people in North America arrived from Asia 20,000 to 12,000 years ago. At that time, the climate was cool and wet. Travelers discovered vast land and rich food sources. Over thousands of years, they settled in certain regions and began farming.

Scientists called archaeologists learn about these early people by digging up their tools and other remains. Some important discoveries have been made in New Mexico. In 1927, archaeologists near Folsom uncovered arrowheads shaped from flint, and the bones of a bison that became extinct 10,000 years ago. In 1932, scientists in Clovis found bones of extinct animals and 12,000-year-old stone weapons. In a cave in western New Mexico, scientists found 5,000-year-old ears of corn. These discoveries showed that the Southwest was one of the first places in North America where people settled.

NEW MEXICO'S FIRST SETTLERS

In the Southwest, the earliest known settlers of the region learned how to grind seeds and nuts into flour. They also made jewelry and pottery. As they developed new and more advanced skills, these settlers became known as the Mogollon people. Historians know that the Mogollon were the first farmers in the region. They established villages and traded goods with other groups.

Over many years, the climate grew warmer and drier. A new human culture emerged, called the Anasazi (a Navajo term that means "Ancient Ones"). The earliest Anasazi, who may have been related to the Mogollon, are sometimes called Basketmakers because they created beautiful baskets. Made from grasses and human hair, these baskets will still hold water without leaking.

The Anasazi began building large villages from about A.D. 800 to 1300. They used stone and adobe (a type of brick made out of thick clay mud that is baked in the sun) to build apartment buildings called pueblos. Each pueblo housed hundreds of people.

Anasazi women carry water to their homes.

The Anasazi hunted deer, elk, antelope, and bighorn sheep. They gathered piñon nuts, yucca fruit, berries, and other wild plants. They also grew food by building irrigation ditches to channel rain to their farmland. The crops and gardens attracted rabbits, birds, and mice. They learned how to store and preserve crops for the winter, and they began raising animals for food. The Anasazi also developed hunting tools and built "roads"—broad pathways that allowed passage between settlements.

Thousands of Anasazi sites have been discovered in New Mexico and Arizona. Two of the most famous are the Aztec Ruins National Monument and Chaco Culture National Historic Park. At the Aztec Ruins (which were incorrectly named after another tribe), one pueblo contains nearly five hundred rooms. Pueblo Bonito, the most impressive structure at Chaco Culture National Historic Park, was once four stories high and had more than six hundred rooms.

The remains of Anasazi buildings are preserved at Aztec Ruins National Monument.

CHANGE AND EXPLORATION

Around 1300, the Anasazi left their homes, heading south or east to other regions. Their great cities stood empty and silent under the desert sun. Why did they abandon their homes? No one knows for sure. Scientists know that a terrible drought struck the area during this time. Maybe their crops were destroyed and they left to find better farmland. Also, wandering groups of another tribe known as the Athapascans (ancestors of today's Navajo and Apache) began raiding the Anasazi settlements. Perhaps the Anasazi left to find a more peaceful place to live.

Whatever happened, Anasazi Pueblo groups eventually settled in other areas of present-day New Mexico. Only one group, the Hopi, established themselves in Arizona. Today, nineteen Pueblo tribes live in New Mexico: the Acoma, Cochiti, Isleta, Jemez, Laguna, Nambé, Picurís, Pojoaque, San Ildefonso, San Felipe, San Juan, Sandia, Santa Ana, Santa Clara, Santo Domingo, Taos, Tesuque, Zía, and Zuñi. The tribes speak several different languages, including Tiwa, Tewa, Keres, and Towa. The Pueblo tribes are located along the Rio Grande valley, stretching from the

The Anasazi may have left their original homeland because of raids on their settlements.

21

northernmost Pueblo of Taos to the southernmost Pueblo of Isleta, and westward to the New Mexico-Arizona border, where the Pueblo of Zuñi is located. The Pueblo tribes are believed to be descended from the Anasazi groups.

THE SPANIARDS ARRIVE

In the 1500s, great changes came to present-day New Mexico. One spring day in 1539, Zuñi people saw a band of strangers approaching them. The leader was a man with skin darker than any they had ever seen. He was a guide named Estevanico de Dorantes, a black slave owned by a Spanish conquistador, or conqueror. These strangers were the first Europeans to arrive in the Southwest.

Estevanico was one of four survivors of a 1528 expedition—a group of men sent to explore what is now Florida. After leaving Florida, the expedition was shipwrecked on the coast of Texas, and the survivors walked more than 1,200 miles (1,920 km) westward across deserts, mountain ranges, and rivers. Estevanico learned to respect and admire the Native Americans they encountered. However, when he approached the Zuñis at the Hawikúh pueblo, the natives attacked the strangers and killed Estevanico. Stories of the attack did not stop the Spaniards from sending even more expeditions to the Southwest.

Why would the Spanish return to this hostile land? They believed they had a mission to convince as many people as possible to become Christians. In addition, a rumor was circulating in Spain about the vast riches of the Seven Cities of Cíbola. These legendary cities were said to be made entirely of gold. In search of the cities, Francisco Vásquez de Coronado led 1,100 men back to the Hawikúh pueblo in 1540. Zuñi weapons were no match for those of the Spanish, who rode in on huge four-legged animals, wore suits made of metal, and used "canes that spit fire and made thunder." (The Native Americans had never seen horses, armor, or guns.)

Coronado never found the cities of gold, and he returned to Mexico City in 1542 greatly disappointed. Still, he had explored and conquered sections of present-day Arizona, New Mexico, Texas, Oklahoma, and Kansas. As a result of Coronado's expedition, the lives of the Pueblos and other Southwest tribes were forever changed.

Coronado was one of the first Europeans to explore the southwestern part of the United States.

THE SPANISH SETTLE IN NEW MEXICO

In 1598, a wealthy Spanish nobleman named Juan de Oñate became governor of the first permanent Spanish colony in New Mexico, named San Juan de los Caballeros, north of present-day Española. It was the first capital of the region the Spaniards called Nuevo Mexico, or New Mexico. Two years later the capital was moved to San Gabriel de Yunque, where the Rio Grande and the Chama River meet.

The Spaniards demanded that Native Americans become Christians, and be loyal to the Spanish king. The Pueblo tribes, especially the Acomas, resented this pressure. Finally, a battle broke out. The Acomas lived in a huge city atop a mesa. Despite its location, the conquistadores still managed to reach the city and slaughter hundreds of Acoma warriors. After this attack, other Pueblos grew even more angry. The Mexican government, too, was angry at Oñate for mistreating the natives and abusing his power, and they ordered him out of San Gabriel.

In 1610, Spain appointed Pedro de Peralta to be the leader of New Mexico. De Peralta moved out of San Gabriel and established new headquarters on the upper

FAMOUS FIRSTS

- Gaspar de Villagra's book, *A History of New Mexico*, was the first book printed about any area of the United States, 1610
- Padre Antonio Jose Martinez printed the first school text in New Mexico, 1793
- The first major gold discovery in the western United States was in the Ortiz Mountains south of Santa Fe, 1828
- New Mexico secretary of state Soledad Chacón became the first American woman to hold a statewide office in 1922, and the first American woman to serve as an acting governor, 1924
- The Gila Wilderness in southwest New Mexico was the first region in America to be set aside by Congress as a national wilderness area, 1924
- New Mexican Octaviano Larrazolo became the first Hispanic American to serve in the United States Senate, 1928
- New Mexico was the first state to have an official cookie, the *biscochito*, adopted in 1989

Santa Fe, founded in 1610, is the oldest capital city in the United States.

Rio Grande. He named the settlement Santa Fe. For a time the Spanish colonists lived peacefully with the Native Americans. The Spanish taught them how to plant crops such as alfalfa, wheat, fruit trees, grapes, and melons. They also brought cattle, sheep, goats, hogs, and horses. In turn, Spaniards learned from Native Americans about corn, piñon nuts, squash, pumpkins, potatoes, cotton, beans, and chiles.

THE PUEBLO REVOLTS

Unfortunately, the peace did not last. Priests began to teach that the Pueblo gods were evil, and soldiers tortured and imprisoned those who refused to become Christians. Angered by the Spaniards, the Native Americans fought back in some villages, such as Jemez and San Felipe.

On August 9, 1680, a Pueblo leader named Popé led hundreds of Native Americans into Santa Fe. During a fierce 9-day battle, the Native Americans drove the Spanish out. Those who escaped fled to El Paso del Norte (now Juarez, Mexico). This battle later became known as the First Pueblo Revolt.

In 1692, officer Diego de Vargas went back to Santa Fe and convinced the Native Americans to allow the Spanish to return to the settlement. Santa Fe still celebrates this peaceful event with an annual fiesta. However, by 1693, when de Vargas returned with many more Spanish families and priests, the Pueblo people had second thoughts

These are the ruins of Pecos Pueblo, site of the Pueblo Revolt.

about allowing the Spanish settlers to return. Instead, they decided to fight. De Vargas took the city by force. After a fierce battle, seventy Native Americans were killed and hundreds were imprisoned. They continued to resist the Spaniards, and in 1696 another war broke out. This war is often called the Second Pueblo Revolt.

CONTINUING STRUGGLES

Over time, Spanish settlers became more accepting of the beliefs and practices of the Native Americans. Throughout the 1700s, however, the colonists fought off attacks by Native American tribes such as the Comanche and Jicarilla Apache, the Navajo, and the Ute, who resented the cultural and other changes the settlers brought to their region. The most powerful tribe was the Comanche, who controlled present-day eastern Colorado, northeastern New Mexico, and western Texas. In 1779, Governor Bautista de Anza led an army against the Comanche. The tribe's most important chief, Cuerno Verde ("Green Horn"), was killed during this battle. Seven years later, the Comanche agreed to sign a peace treaty with Spain.

Despite these problems, Spanish settlements continued to expand. San Felipe de Alburquerque, near present-day Albuquerque, was settled in 1706. The Mexican government encouraged settlers to move outside the Rio Grande valley by offering land to those who agreed to live there and farm it. As a result, villas such as Santa Rosa de Lima, San Miguel del Vado, and Belen were settled.

A group of emigrants sets up camp along the Santa Fe Trail during the early 19th century.

In 1821, Mexico declared independence from Spain. As a result, New Mexico became part of the Mexican Republic. The new nation was eager to trade with foreigners, especially with the United States. An American trader named William Becknell traveled east on a rugged supply route to report the news about Mexico's independence. A year later, he and some other traders left Missouri for Santa Fe along the same trail. Missouri was a new state and needed gold and silver from Mexico to help its economy grow. It was cheaper and easier for northern Mexico to trade with Missouri merchants than to import, or bring in, goods from Mexico City. This trade route between Independence, Missouri, and Santa Fe became known as the Santa Fe Trail.

Most of the expeditions that ended or began in New Mexico were made up of merchants who traveled to Missouri to obtain goods to sell once they returned home. Others originated in Missouri, where merchants brought goods to sell in New Mexico. Mining, sheep herding, farming, construction, and Native American craft-making (such as weaving and jewelry-making) were among the chief occupations of New Mexicans during this century.

Trade increased so much on the Santa Fe Trail that a stagecoach line was begun in 1850. For most of the 1800s, the Santa Fe Trail was one of the most important routes to the West and Mexico, especially for gold, silver, wool, cotton and other fabrics, and supplies for the United States Army. The trail was 800 miles (1,287 km) long.

NEW MEXICO AND THE UNITED STATES

By 1846 the United States wanted more land. That year, the United States declared war against Mexico and took possession of New Mexico by marching across its northern border, which was not protected. The Mexican–American War ended in 1848, and the United States gained control of a huge territory, including New Mexico.

On September 9, 1850, the United States created New Mexico Territory. It included present-day New Mexico, Arizona, southern Colorado, southern Utah, and part of southeastern Nevada. The territory was divided in 1863, and the western half became Arizona Territory.

In 1861, war broke out between the northern states and the southern states. During the Civil War (1861–1865), New Mexico was the scene of several battles. Soldiers from Texas invaded New Mexico Territory in 1861 and captured Santa Fe and Albuquerque. The fighting in New Mexico lasted only about a year, but it left more than 1,300 people dead.

WHAT'S IN A NAME?

The names of several places in New Mexico have interesting origins.

Name	Comes From or Means
Albuquerque	Named for Viceroy Francisco Fernandez de la Cueva, Duke of Alburquerque (The first r in Alburquerque was later dropped.)
Clovis	Named for a French king, Clovis I
Gallup	Named for David L. Gallup, paymaster for the Atlantic and Pacific Railroad
Roswell	First name of the father of Van Smith, who settled present-day Roswell
Taos	One of the Pueblo tribes who inhabited the area before the arrival of European explorers

Christopher "Kit" Carson (1809–1868) was a frontiersman and soldier who lived in Santa Fe and Taos. Because he was so familiar with the Southwest, Carson served as a guide on many exploring expeditions in the area. During the Civil War, most of his military actions were directed against Native Americans, who were forced to leave their home territories under Carson's orders.

One of the most famous frontiersmen of this period was Christopher "Kit" Carson. He was a native of Kentucky who helped organize and command the 1st New Mexican Volunteers during the Civil War. The 1st New Mexican soldiers engaged in campaigns against the Apache, Navajo, and Comanche tribes in New Mexico and Texas. When the war ended, Carson was promoted to brigadier general and placed in command of Fort Garland, Colorado.

During the 1800s, the United States government made peace treaties with Native American groups. The government also set up special areas for them called reservations. After the Civil War, the government began forcing Native Americans to relocate to the reservations so that it could make room for white settlers. The most famous forced relocation in New Mexico is known as the Long Walk. In 1864, about 8,000 Navajo and Apache were driven out of their homelands in northeastern Arizona and northwestern New Mexico. They were forced to walk to Bosque Redondo, about 300 miles (440 km) away. Thousands of Native Americans died of starvation and disease along the way. After four years, the government finally permitted them to return home.

During this period, the United States grew quickly. Railroad companies raced to connect far-flung western territories with the populous eastern states and open the territories to settlement. Soon the Southwest echoed with the sounds of railroad tracks being laid and trains steaming through. The railroad reached Santa Fe in 1880. Railroads helped farmers, ranchers, miners, and lumbermen, and all the people who made a living serving them.

The quick expansion also created problems. After Mexican independence from Spain in 1821, New Mexico was opened to trade with foreigners for the first time, espe-

Railroads opened up parts of New Mexico for further development.

cially along the Santa Fe Trail. As the number of settlers increased, so did the number of drifters, gamblers, cattle thieves, and other criminals. The American frontier at this time is often called "the Wild West," because the United States government could afford few lawmen (known as marshals) to patrol its western territories. Outlaws such as Billy the Kid thrived in the lawless atmosphere.

In 1910, President William H. Taft allowed New Mexico to write a constitution in preparation for statehood. (A constitution is a document that outlines rules and a form of government.) Voters approved New Mexico's constitution in January, 1911. The following year, the president admitted New Mexico, with a population of 327,300, as the forty-seventh state in the Union. "Well, it is all over," Taft said to the New Mexican delegates gathered before him. "I am glad to give you life. I hope you will be healthy." A few days later, the first governor of the new state, William C. McDonald, was sworn in. McDonald served until 1916. Santa Fe became the official capital of the state.

EXTRA! EXTRA!

William H. "Billy the Kid" Bonney (shown above) was a famous cattle thief in New Mexico Territory. The teenager killed several men before he was captured and sentenced to death, but he escaped. Sheriff Pat Garrett recaptured him in 1880, but Billy escaped once again. Three months later, however, the sheriff found and killed him.

STATEHOOD

New Mexico faced a bright future. Artists and craftspeople from the East and the Midwest began traveling to New Mexico, especially to Taos. A group of these newcomers formed the Taos Society of Artists. The area became a haven for poets, painters, and novelists. Taos is still a well-known artist colony today.

WHO'S WHO IN NEW MEXICO?

Georgia O'Keeffe (1887–1986) was one of New Mexico's most famous residents. She was an artist known for her "close-up" paintings of flowers and her strong Southwestern interest. She lived in Ghost Ranch and Abiquiu.

The newly formed state was still shaping its government when World War I (1914–1918) broke out in 1914. The United States did not enter the war until 1917. In February that year, the United States government discovered a secret message from Germany to Mexico. Germany, led by Kaiser (emperor) Wilhelm II, was proposing an alliance with Mexico. In return for their help, Germany offered to recover Mexico's former territories in Texas, New Mexico, and Arizona, and return them to Mexico. The message implied that Germany was prepared to wage war against the United States. As a result, in April 1917 the United States joined with France, England, and other countries to fight against Germany and Austria-Hungary in Europe.

Difficult times followed in the 1930s, when the Great Depression affected all of America. Jobs were scarce and people had little money. New Mexico was hard-hit. Many of its mines and railroads closed. Cattle ranches grew smaller and ranchers let employees go. "Towns" of ramshackle huts arose on the outskirts of larger cities, as newly homeless people looked for work.

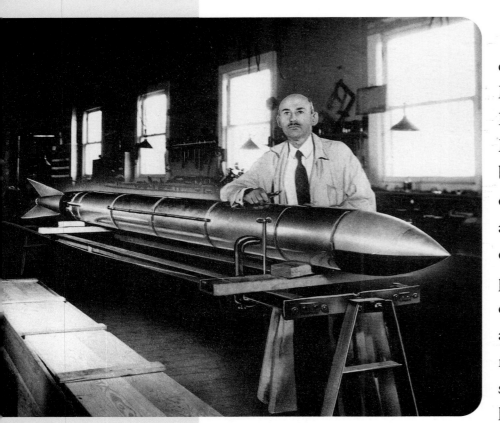

Robert Goddard worked in a laboratory near Roswell to develop his rockets.

This period was also one of discovery and experimentation. A Massachusetts scientist named Robert Goddard came to New Mexico to test his rockets. He believed that the vast, unpopulated desert region of the state would be an ideal place to experiment without causing damage or harming people. Although the rockets (also called missiles) were quite small—about the size of today's "model" rockets—Goddard believed that someday people would launch huge vehicles into space. Most people thought he was foolish, but Goddard was far ahead of his time. He and other scientists helped New Mexico become a leader in the country's space program.

World War II (1939–1945) helped end the Great Depression. As the United States began producing more goods to ship to countries involved in the war, its economy quickly improved. In 1941, the United States entered World War II, fighting against Germany and Japan with its allies, France, Britain, and Russia. Two regiments (large groups of soldiers) from New Mexico suffered terribly in the Philippines after they were captured by Japanese forces. About 1,800 men endured what is known as the Bataan Death March, a forced journey of 65 miles (105 km) to prison camps. Those who did not die on the march spent 40 months in the camps. Fewer than 900 men made it back to America, and about 300 more died within a year of returning home. Altogether, more than 60,000 New Mexicans served in the United States Armed Forces during World War II.

Other New Mexicans also helped defeat the Japanese and Germans. The Navajo and the Apache passed messages from one general or regiment to another, using their native languages. The idea of doing so originated with a man named Philip Johnston, the son of a missionary to the Navajo. He grew up on a Navajo reservation and was one of the few non-natives who spoke the language fluently. The Navajo language is unwritten and has no alphabet. It is extremely complex and is only spoken in the Navajo lands of the Southwest. The Apache language is equally complex. Using these languages, "code talkers" helped to confuse enemy forces that were secretly listening.

The atomic bomb was secretly developed at Los Alamos, in an abandoned school for boys.

During the war, New Mexico achieved another kind of fame. In 1943, a group of scientists arrived at a secluded ranch in Los Alamos, west of Santa Fe. Neighbors were puzzled as they watched more and more strangers traveling to the old ranch. The scientists were secretly working for the United

States government to develop the deadliest weapon in history—the atomic bomb. They had chosen this remote area to avoid attention and to be clear of heavily populated areas. The research was called the Manhattan Project, and the project's leader was Robert Oppenheimer. On July 16, 1945, near Alamogordo, the scientists huddled in protected areas and watched as the first atomic bomb was detonated (set off). The explosion shattered windows in Silver City, 120 miles (190 km) away. The blinding ball of light produced in the blast could be seen in Santa Fe, almost 300 miles (440 km) away. The blast created temperatures so high that nearby sand melted into glass. In August, 1945, the United States dropped these bombs on two cities in Japan—Hiroshima and Nagasaki. The bombings put an end to World War II.

People as far away as Santa Fe saw the brilliant light of the atomic bomb detonation near Alamogordo in July 1945.

Nuclear testing, such as that done for the atomic bomb, later provided great benefits for New Mexico. Sandia National Laboratories and the White Sands Missile Range, both centers of testing and research, have contributed millions of dollars to the state's economy. Sandia National Laboratories drew so many new employees that Albuquerque doubled in size within ten years. Still, some citizens were concerned. This type of scientific research was new and dangerous, and they feared what might happen if an explosion or accident occurred.

FIND OUT MORE

In 1947, New Mexico made national headlines when some people claimed they saw a UFO (Unidentified Flying Object) crash between Roswell and Corona. Roswell still celebrates its strange reputation by holding "alien" festivals and selling souvenirs. Some people believe the UFO sightings were real. Others think that people must have seen some special airplanes the government was testing, or even just tricks of the sunlight. What do you think people saw?

MODERN NEW MEXICO

In the 1960s, New Mexico suffered from great unrest. When the United States took possession of New Mexico in the mid-1800s, the government signed a treaty that promised Hispanic landowners that they could keep their property. The government also promised residents (who were formerly Mexican citizens) that it would protect their civil rights and

their property. The United States government did not follow through on its promise, however. As time passed, Hispanics and Mexicans living in the region began losing their property as the government seized it for its own purposes.

In 1967, a Mexican-American named Reies Tijerina attempted to forcibly take back some of the land taken by the government and return it to Hispanics. Tijerina and his followers raided a courthouse at Tierra Amarilla and took two hostages, who later escaped. The governor called in the National Guard to settle the unrest. Tijerina was arrested and imprisoned. Still, the debate continues. For hundreds of years, the citizens of New Mexico have struggled to decide who will own and control the land.

In the 1980s, the United States government gave almost $2 billion to companies in New Mexico to develop weapons for use in space. This was called the "Star Wars" program. Some residents argued that the money would have been better used helping New Mexico's poor people. In the end, the

WHO'S WHO IN NEW MEXICO?

Dionisio (Dennis) Chavez (1888–1962) was a United States representative of New Mexico from 1931 to 1935. He became a United States senator in 1935 and served until his death. Chavez supported the rights of Native Americans and Hispanic Americans. He helped establish the federal Fair Employment Practices Commission, which aims to stop discrimination in workplaces. Discrimination is the unfair treatment of people based on their belonging to a certain race or group.

project was never fully developed. But the American space program again put New Mexico in the spotlight, at least briefly. The space shuttle *Columbia* ended its third mission by landing safely at White Sands Missile Range near Alamogordo on March 30, 1982.

Events in the 1990s celebrated New Mexico's rich cultural history. In 1992, the state observed the Columbus Quincentenary (500-year anniversary), remembering Christopher Columbus's discovery of the New World. Although Columbus was born in Italy, his expeditions were funded by King Ferdinand and Queen Isabella of Spain, and he claimed the land he discovered on Spain's behalf. His direct descendant, Cristobal Colon XX, was welcomed at the 1992 celebration. In 1998, the state celebrated the 400th anniversary of the founding of Santa Fe by Juan de Oñate.

These celebrations caused some controversy. Some people believe that the Spanish explorers should not be honored because of the way many of them mistreated Native Americans. Others argue that the celebrations honor the way three cultures—Hispanic, Native American, and Anglo—have learned to live together. Thomas Chávez, who writes for the *Santa Fe New Mexican,* reminded his readers that the state flag shows a union of cultures. The sun

A festival in Santa Fe celebrates the Spanish heritage of New Mexico. This man is dressed as a Spanish conquistador.

symbol of the Zia tribe is red and yellow, the colors of Spain. "New Mexico is a story of survival," Mr. Chávez wrote. "It is a legacy with a lesson, for the people involved with this story learned . . . to live with each other despite disagreements and disruptions and, over time, have learned that we are better off as a result."

CHAPTER FOUR

GOVERNING NEW MEXICO

On November 21, 1910, the United States government asked New Mexico to draft a constitution in preparation for statehood. A constitution is a document that outlines rules and a form of government. The constitution was officially adopted on January 21, 1911, and New Mexico became a state in 1912. Since then, state lawmakers have made hundreds of changes, called amendments, to the state constitution.

Like the United States government, the New Mexico state government has three parts: the legislative branch, the executive branch, and the judicial branch. The legislative branch makes the laws. The executive branch carries out the laws. The judicial branch interprets the laws. These branches "check" on one another, so that no branch gains too much power.

Built in 1966, New Mexico's state capitol is one of the newest capitol buildings in the country.

New Mexico's legislative branch has two parts—the house of representatives and the senate. In New Mexico, the house of representatives has 70 members, who each serve 2-year terms. The senate has 42 members, who are elected to 4-year terms. Members of the legislature hold meetings to discuss proposed new laws (called bills), such as those that set aside funds to pay for schools or to build new roads. After legislators discuss and approve a bill, they send the final copy to the governor. A bill becomes a law when the governor signs it.

The New Mexico legislature meets in the capitol building.

The New Mexico legislature meets in Santa Fe, the state capital, each year for 30 or 60 days. The governor may issue a proclamation calling for a special session. In special sessions, legislators may discuss only the work named in the governor's proclamation.

EXECUTIVE BRANCH

The head of the executive branch is the governor, who is elected by the people of New Mexico. The governor serves for 4 years. He or she may sign bills into law or veto (reject) them. The governor appoints non-elected officials to serve in other government offices and grants pardons (official documents granting release) for certain types of crimes. He or

Inside the state capitol, the state seal appears on the floor of the lobby.

she also prepares the state budget, which determines how the state's money will be spent. The governor also issues emergency orders during a disaster, and may call out the state militia (the state's armed forces) to help keep the peace.

Other members of the executive branch include the lieutenant governor, the secretary of state, the auditor, the treasurer, the attorney general, and the commissioner of public lands. All of these officials are elected to 4-year terms. They may be re-elected once, though not consecutively.

NEW MEXICO GOVERNORS

Name	Term	Name	Term
William C. McDonald	1912–1917	John F. Simms, Jr.	1955–1957
Ezequiel C. de Baca	1917	Edwin L. Mechem	1957–1959
Washington E. Lindsey	1917–1919	John Burroughs	1959–1961
Octaviano A. Larrazolo	1919–1921	Edwin L. Mechem	1961–1962
Merritt C. Mechem	1921–1923	Tom Bolack	1962–1963
James F. Hinkle	1923–1925	Jack M. Campbell	1963–1967
Arthur T. Hannett	1925–1927	David F. Cargo	1967–1971
Richard C. Dillon	1927–1931	Bruce King	1971–1975
Arthur Seligman	1931–1933	Jerry Apodaca	1975–1979
Andrew D. Hockenhull	1933–1935	Bruce King	1979–1983
Clyde Tingley	1935–1939	Toney Anaya	1983–1987
John E. Miles	1939–1943	Garrey Carruthers	1987–1991
John J. Dempsey	1943–1947	Bruce King	1991–1995
Thomas J. Mabry	1947–1951	Gary E. Johnson	1995–2003
Edwin L. Mechem	1951–1955	Bill Richardson	2003–present

New Mexico's judicial branch consists of seven types of courts. The supreme court of New Mexico is the highest or most important court, with the final say over all cases. It has the power to decide whether a law goes against the state constitution. If it does, that law is declared unconstitutional and is no longer a law. New Mexico's supreme court has 5 judges. The supreme court is located in Santa Fe.

The second type of court is the court of appeals, with 10 judges. The court of appeals hears some cases that have already been tried in lower courts to determine if the cases were tried fairly. If a person is not satisfied with the outcome of his or her case in a lower court, they may request a new trial before the court of appeals.

The third type, district court, has 72 judges in 13 districts. In the fourth type, called magistrate court, 61 judges handle cases involving traffic violations and minor crimes. The fifth type is municipal (city) courts. There are 83 municipal courts in New Mexico. The sixth type is probate court. One judge in each of New Mexico's 33 counties hears cases about wills. A will is a document that explains how a person wants to distribute his or her money and possessions after death.

The seventh type of court in New Mexico is a metropolitan court. Only one such court exists in New Mexico—the Bernalillo County Metropolitan Court. It has 16 judges, who may be elected or appointed by the governor. Thirteen of these judges hear certain types of criminal complaints called misdemeanors (crimes for which the maximum penalty is less than one year in jail and less than

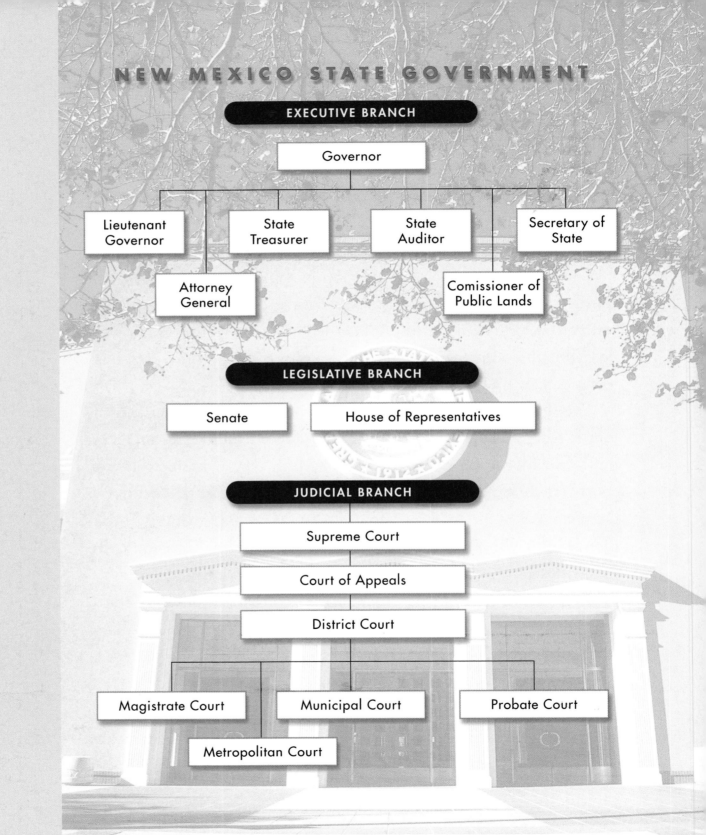

NEW MEXICO STATE GOVERNMENT

EXECUTIVE BRANCH

Governor

Lieutenant Governor

State Treasurer

State Auditor

Secretary of State

Attorney General

Comissioner of Public Lands

LEGISLATIVE BRANCH

Senate

House of Representatives

JUDICIAL BRANCH

Supreme Court

Court of Appeals

District Court

Magistrate Court

Municipal Court

Probate Court

Metropolitan Court

$1,000 in fines). The other three judges hear civil complaints (cases involving personal civil rights). Each metropolitan court judge serves a 4-year term.

TAKE A TOUR OF SANTA FE, THE STATE CAPITAL

Santa Fe is geographically one of the smallest state capitals in the United States. It is also the third most heavily populated city in New Mexico, with 62,203 residents. The city sits atop a plateau that rises 7,000 feet (2,135 m) above sea level, making it America's highest state capital as well.

Walking through Santa Fe is like taking a trip through New Mexico's history. Located in the center of Santa Fe is the Plaza, the square that was laid out by Governor Pedro de Peralta in 1610. In the past, this area was used mainly for soldiers to practice marching, but also for fiestas (celebrations) and bullfights. It marked the end of the Santa Fe Trail. Today, the Plaza is lined with shops, art galleries, and restaurants. It is still the heart of the city.

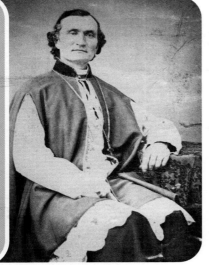
On the northern side of the Plaza is the Palace of the Governors, one of the oldest public buildings in the United States. In 1909, the Palace of the Governors became the headquarters for the Museum of New Mexico. In the shaded area under the arches of the palace, Native Americans sell handmade crafts and jewelry, as they have done for centuries. Today you can go inside the palace and see the History Museum. Across the street is the Museum of Fine Arts. Two other state museums sit on a hill overlooking the city.

If you walk a block east, you'll find the beautiful Cathedral of St. Francis of Assisi. Santa Fe's first archbishop, Jean Baptiste Lamy, founded the church. Inside a chapel on the northeast side of the church is a statue of the Madonna that Diego de Vargas carried into Santa Fe in 1692.

Head south from the Palace of the Governors and cross the Santa Fe River to arrive at the Mission of San Miguel of Santa Fe. This church is the oldest one still in use in the United States. It has an 800-pound (363-kilogram) bell that was cast in 1356 in Spain.

A block south of this church is the modern capitol building, which was completed in 1966. The building is round with four branches leading from its center, the same shape as the Zia sun symbol, which also appears on the state flag. You can visit the Governor's Gallery or stroll

The Mission of San Miguel was rebuilt in 1710. It is believed that the original structure was destroyed by fire during the First Pueblo Revolt.

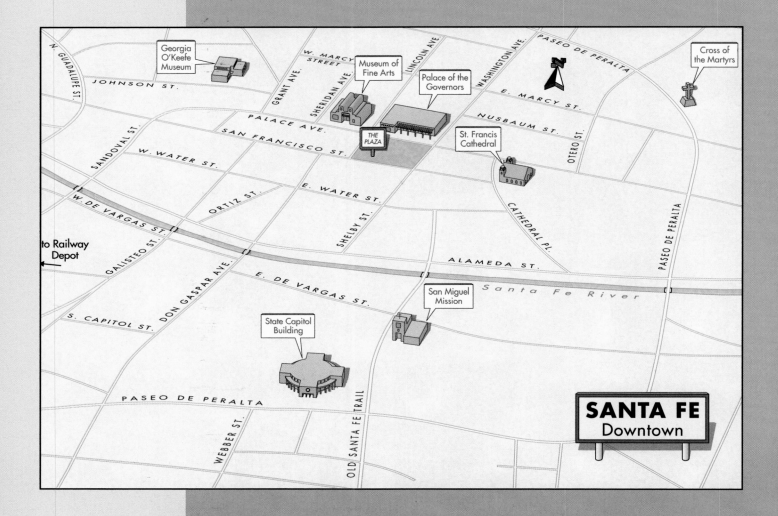

SANTA FE
Downtown

through six acres (2.4 ha) of beautiful gardens containing plum and almond trees, roses, and sequoias.

Northeast of Santa Fe's center is a hill on which you can see an enormous white cross. This is the Cross of the Martyrs, which honors 23 Franciscan monks who were killed by Native Americans during the first Pueblo Revolt. On Guadalupe Street, near the Santuario de Nuestra Señora de Guadalupe, you can board a train and ride the Burlington Northern Santa Fe Railway. This 120-year-old route passes through scenic desert land and ends in Lamy, 18 miles (29 km) south of Santa Fe. It's the same route that once carried settlers, adventurers, and artists to and from the state capital.

The Burlington Northern Santa Fe Railway still carries people—and freight—through parts of New Mexico.

CHAPTER FIVE

THE PEOPLE AND PLACES OF NEW MEXICO

Spanish dancers perform at El Rancho de las Golondrinas, a museum dedicated to the Hispanic culture of New Mexico.

According to the 2000 census, New Mexicans numbered 1,819,046—an increase of almost one-fourth since 1990. Yet the state ranks thirty-sixth in population among all the states. If everyone in New Mexico were spread out evenly, there would be 15 people per square mile (6 per sq km). This figure is known as its population density. In contrast, New Jersey has 1,135 people per square mile (438 per sq km). New Mexico is also a "young" state: 42 of every 100 New Mexicans are between 20 and 49 years old.

The three largest ethnic groups in New Mexico are Anglo-Americans, Hispanic Americans, and Native Americans. These groups overlap. For example, a person may be both Hispanic and Native American, or may have both Anglo and Hispanic ancestors. About 67 of every 100 people are "Anglos," or non-Hispanic Caucasians.

Hispanic people may trace their roots to Spain, Mexico, Latin America, or some South American nations. Hispanics make up 42 of every 100 people in New Mexico, the highest of any state. New Mexico's Native American population is also high compared to other states: almost 1 in every 10 people is Native American. Two of every 100 New Mexicans are African-American.

New Mexico is the only state in which two languages—English and Spanish—are officially recognized by the state constitution. In a few villages, people speak a 400-year-old version of Spanish. Some Native

A Native American woman and child bake bread at San Ildefonso Pueblo.

Americans in New Mexico speak as many as four languages—their own language, some Spanish and English, and perhaps another tribal tongue.

WORKING IN NEW MEXICO

Most of the population and job growth in New Mexico is in the areas surrounding Albuquerque, Las Cruces, and Santa Fe. More workers are employed in nonfarming jobs than ever before, and most nonfarming jobs are in cities. Building and construction, service industries (including education), and the state government account for most nonfarming jobs in New Mexico.

One of the largest employers in the state is Wal-Mart, a chain of retail stores, which employs more than 9,000 people. Retail is the largest type of business in the state, employing more than 116,000 New Mexicans. Another 20,000 work in the wholesale trade, meaning that they work as suppliers for products that are resold in retail stores.

New Mexico's factories employ 53,000 people. Intel, a computer-chip manufacturer, is one of the largest factory employers in the state. Among the fastest-growing industries is the construction business, which employs almost 47,000 people and grew by 4 percent between 2000 and 2001.

More than 15,500 residents of New Mexico work in mining. Uranium, copper, and potash are some of the natural resources mined in New Mexico. The state is also one of the top producers of natural gas. Another 20,500 people work in agriculture, forestry, and fishing.

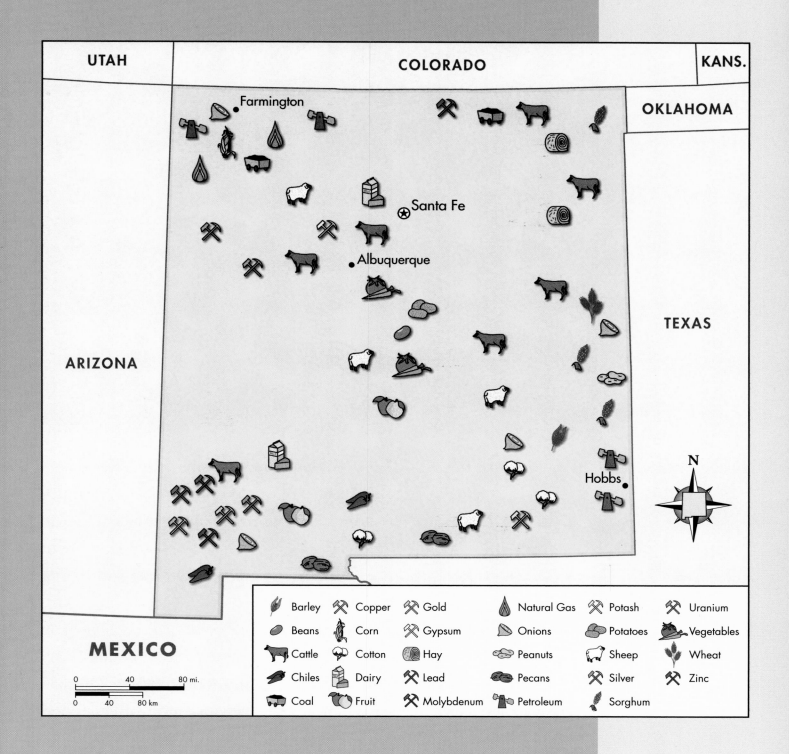

UTAH

COLORADO

KANS.

OKLAHOMA

Farmington

Santa Fe

Albuquerque

ARIZONA

TEXAS

Hobbs

N

MEXICO

0 40 80 mi.

0 40 80 km

Barley	Copper	Gold	Natural Gas	Potash	Uranium
Beans	Corn	Gypsum	Onions	Potatoes	Vegetables
Cattle	Cotton	Hay	Peanuts	Sheep	Wheat
Chiles	Dairy	Lead	Pecans	Silver	Zinc
Coal	Fruit	Molybdenum	Petroleum	Sorghum	

Potash, which is mined in New Mexico, is primarily used to make fertilizer for crops.

New Mexico is a hub of development in weapons and nuclear energy for the United States government. A great number of New Mexicans work in research. Another important industry is optics products. These products include polished mirrors for telescopes and laser equipment used in satellites. Still other New Mexicans work for companies that invent and produce medicines.

New Mexico's economy is still based largely on agriculture. The state has more than 14,000 farms and sells $1.6 billion of farm products each year. What do you think is New Mexico's top farm product? Did you guess chiles? New Mexico is America's biggest producer of chiles and

A woman sorts through a tub of red chiles, a common ingredient in many South-western dishes.

Emmi Whitehorse (1957–) is a Native American artist. She creates abstract paintings using traditional colors of the Southwest and elements of her Navajo background. She lives in Santa Fe.

summer onions. Other important crops are peanuts, pecans, sorghum, sweet corn, melons, cotton and cottonseed, and wheat.

Tourism is an important business in New Mexico. Tourism is the business of providing food, entertainment, and shelter to visitors. In 2000, more than 4 million people flocked to the state's 14 national parks and monuments and 5 national forests. New Mexico's numerous art, science, nature, culture, and history museums also draw crowds of visitors. Many tourists buy Native American crafts as souvenirs. Navajo blankets, rugs, pottery, and silver and turquoise jewelry are some of the products you can buy. More than 9,000 New Mexicans work in the tourist industry.

A Native American woman displays her crafts for visitors at the Pueblo Cultural Center.

This recipe makes the licorice-flavored official cookie of New Mexico. *Biscochitos* are often served at weddings, baptisms, and holiday parties. The number of cookies you get depends on how big you make them! Don't forget to ask an adult for help.

BISCOCHITOS

1 1/4 cups margarine, softened
2 eggs
1/4 teaspoon salt
1 1/2 teaspoons baking powder
4 cups flour
1 cup sugar
1 tablespoon powdered anise or anise seeds
1 tablespoon rum flavoring (if desired)
1 cup water or milk
cinnamon and sugar mixture for topping (mix 1 cup sugar with 2-3 tsp. cinnamon)

1. Preheat oven to 350°F.
2. Beat eggs in a small bowl.
3. In a large bowl, mix all remaining ingredients except cinnamon and sugar mixture. Add beaten eggs.
4. When mixture feels like a soft dough, use a rolling pin to flatten it until it is about 1/4 in (1/2 cm) thick.
5. Cut flattened dough into shapes using a table knife or cookie cutters. Traditional *biscochito* designs are bows or fleurs-de-lis (like a flower with three petals), but you can make any shape.
6. Arrange shapes on a cookie sheet. Bake approximately fifteen minutes or until light brown.
7. Sprinkle with cinnamon and sugar mixture while still warm. Cool on a wire rack.

The message on this rock dates from 1605.

Northwest and North Central New Mexico

A good place to begin a tour is El Malpais National Conservation Area. There you can view lava flows and other volcanic formations. You can also visit Inscription Rock, a 200-foot (61-m) sandstone mesa named *El Morro* ("The Bluff"). Ancient tribes carved pictures and writings into this rock. In 1605, Juan de Oñate left his name and the date. You can still read most of these markings. Not far from *El Morro* is the Bandera Volcano and Ice Cave. The cave was created 5,000 years ago when lava flowed from a volcano and carved "tubes" into the land. The tubes gradually collapsed as the lava cooled. Water that flowed into the cave and froze thousands of years ago has never melted.

In the northwest corner of New Mexico is the towering Shiprock. This unusual rock formation resembles a ship with billowing sails.

Northwest New Mexico is the home of many of the state's Native Americans. It was also where the mysterious Anasazi people lived. You can see the remains of their homes and villages at the Aztec Ruins National Monument, the Bandelier National Monument, and Chaco Culture National Historic Park.

The Four Corners Monument lies at the juncture of the Utah, Colorado, New Mexico, and Arizona borders. At Four Corners, you can be in four states at once. How? Stand with one foot in each of two states, then bend over and place your hands in the other two!

Forty of every 100 New Mexicans live in the north-central region, from Albuquerque to Santa Fe and Los Alamos. Another major city is Taos, which is actually three villages. The oldest of these is the Taos Pueblo, whose main buildings are 900 years old. The second is the Spanish town settled in 1615. The third is Ranchos de Taos, a farming community with a famous mission church. Today, Taos is a popular ski area.

Taos Pueblo looks today almost exactly as it did when Coronado saw it in the 1500s.

FIND OUT MORE

New Mexico has as many as 130 "ghost towns." These are settlements that were started in the late 1800s but were later abandoned. Mogollon is a ghost town 75 miles (121 km) northwest of Silver City. Why might people have settled in this area? Why do you think they abandoned the towns?

In southwestern New Mexico you will find Elephant Butte Reservoir. This is an artificial lake created by a dam of the Rio Grande in 1916. It is 40 miles (64 km) long with more than 200 miles (322 km) of shoreline. Millions of years ago, this area was a huge, shallow ocean where dinosaurs roamed in search of food. Today, the lakeshore is a popular spot for water sports.

Just north of Elephant Butte is the Bosque del Apache National Wildlife Refuge, a favorite of birdwatchers and a refuge for the endangered whooping crane. Every November, the refuge hosts a 4-day event called the Festival of Cranes. During the festival, visitors can take guided tours of areas not usually open to the public.

About 40 miles (63 km) north of Silver City, you can visit the Gila Cliff Dwellings, five natural caves in the face of a cliff. The cliff rises 175 feet (53 m) above the canyon floor. The Mogollon people carved the dwellings 700 years ago. You can also see "pit houses" that are nearly 2,000 years old.

About 50 miles (80 km) west of Socorro on Route 60 is the Very Large Array (VLA) Radio Astronomy Observatory. The VLA uses 27 huge, dish-shaped antennas to collect radio waves from planets, stars, and galaxies. The VLA is the largest radio-telescope array in the world. You can see it in the 1997 film *Contact*, which starred Jodie Foster as an astronomer.

Central New Mexico

In central New Mexico you can see the remains of old frontier trails. El Camino Real linked pueblos and Spanish settlements. Follow the Jemez Mountain Trail to visit Pueblo ruins and amazing natural formations such as Battleship Rock, a steep cliff that resembles the bow of a mighty ship.

The data collected by the Very Large Array is used by astronomers throughout the world.

Settlers who came seeking gold during the 1800s discovered a beautiful blue stone called turquoise, and they named their route the Turquoise Trail. Along this trail are many old mining towns and tourist shops.

Albuquerque rests in a valley between the Sandia Mountains and the Colorado Plateau. Central Avenue in Albuquerque is part of historic Route 66. It ran 2,448 miles (3,940 km) from Chicago, Illinois, to Santa Monica, California, until major interstate highways replaced it. Only parts of the route are visible today.

While traveling the Turquoise Trail you'll see this church in Golden, an old mining town.

Petroglyphs such as this one tell the story of the Pueblo peoples.

Two of New Mexico's most amazing national monuments are near Albuquerque. The Petroglyph National Monument on the western border of the city contains 17 miles (27 km) of mesas and 25,000 Native American and Hispanic petroglyphs (images carved in rock). The Salinas Pueblo Missions National Monument, about 50 miles (80 km) south of Albuquerque, spans 1,071 acres (433 ha) and contains three pueblos. During the 1600s, this valley was a busy Pueblo trade center.

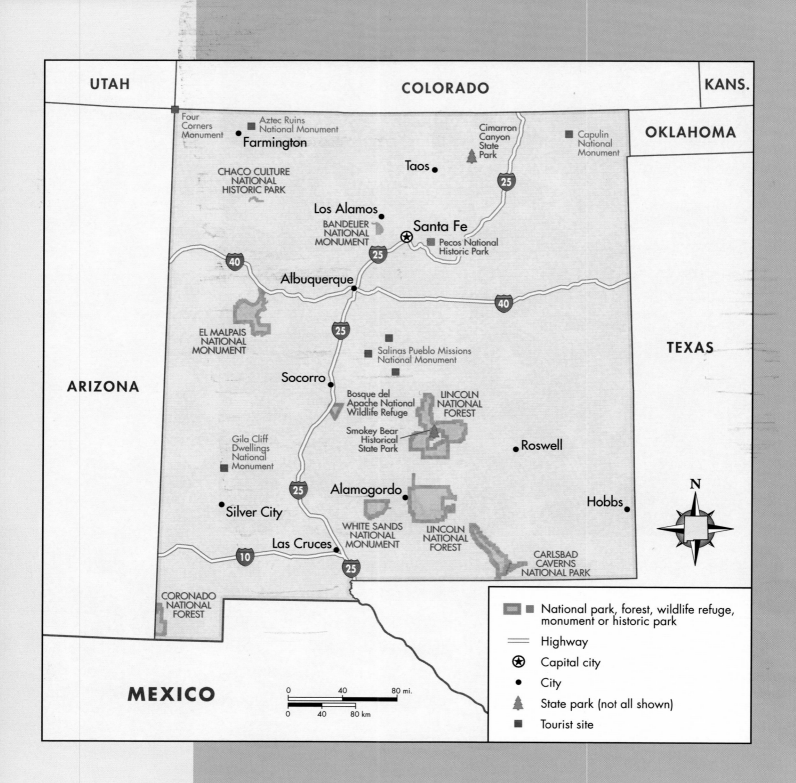

UTAH
COLORADO
KANS.
OKLAHOMA

Four Corners Monument
Aztec Ruins National Monument
Capulin National Monument
Farmington
Cimarron Canyon State Park
CHACO CULTURE NATIONAL HISTORIC PARK
Taos
25
Los Alamos
BANDELIER NATIONAL MONUMENT
⊛ Santa Fe
Pecos National Historic Park
25
40
Albuquerque
40
EL MALPAIS NATIONAL MONUMENT
25
Salinas Pueblo Missions National Monument
TEXAS
ARIZONA
Socorro
Bosque del Apache National Wildlife Refuge
LINCOLN NATIONAL FOREST
Gila Cliff Dwellings National Monument
Smokey Bear Historical State Park
Roswell
25
Alamogordo
Silver City
Hobbs
WHITE SANDS NATIONAL MONUMENT
LINCOLN NATIONAL FOREST
N
Las Cruces
25
CARLSBAD CAVERNS NATIONAL PARK
10
CORONADO NATIONAL FOREST
MEXICO

0   40   80 mi.
0   40   80 km

National park, forest, wildlife refuge, monument or historic park
Highway
⊛ Capital city
• City
State park (not all shown)
■ Tourist site

Northeast New Mexico

Among the natural wonders in the northeast is Cimarron Canyon State Park, a fishing and camping area with 400-foot (122-m) rock formations. A volcano that erupted ten thousand years ago is now the center of the nearby Capulin National Monument. Also along the Santa Fe Trail, southeast of the state capital, is the Pecos National Historical Park. You can tour the remains of the Pecos pueblo and two Spanish missions there.

Southeast New Mexico

The southeast is where legends about the Wild West were born. You can also see White Sands National Monument and the Carlsbad Caverns there. The Carlsbad Caverns are the most popular tourist attraction in the state. This huge system of limestone caves contains more than 30 miles (48 km) of rooms and hallways. It was formed between 250 and 200 million years ago by an inland sea that covered the southwest part of the United States. You can tour about 3 miles (4.8 km) of the caverns. You'll enter through a natural opening 90 feet (27 m) wide and 40 feet (12 m) high, or take an elevator down into the caverns.

The Lincoln National Forest has a unique claim to fame. The original "Smokey Bear" was a New Mexico black bear cub found clinging to a charred tree after a fire devastated Lincoln National Forest in 1950. Now Smokey is a mascot for a nationwide fire prevention campaign.

FIND OUT MORE

In many areas along what was once the Santa Fe Trail, you can still see "swales," or ruts made by wagon wheels. Think about the climate of New Mexico where the swales appear. Why do you think they are visible today despite many years of weather and erosion?

The Carlsbad Caverns were formed over millions of years by water that carved its way through limestone bedrock.

You can visit the site where Smokey is buried (he died in 1976) at the Smokey Bear Historical State Park in Capitan.

A LAND OF MANY HISTORIES

New Mexico is an ancient land that was settled first by Native Americans, later by Spanish explorers, and finally by pioneers from the eastern United States and other countries. People still travel to New Mexico to find jobs in nuclear research and electronics. Side by side with booming cities like Albuquerque are dusty ghost towns and old Spanish missions that remind visitors of the state's fascinating history and culture. Now that you know more about New Mexico, it is easy to see how it earned the nickname "Land of Enchantment."

NEW MEXICO ALMANAC

Statehood date and number: January 6, 1912; 47th state

State seal: Adopted 1887, modified 1912

State flag: A red Zia Pueblo sun symbol on a field of yellow, adopted 1925

Geographic center: Torrence (12 miles south-southwest of Willard)

Total area/rank: 121,598 square miles (314,937 sq km)/5th

Borders: Oklahoma, Texas, Colorado, Arizona, Utah, and Mexico

Latitude and longitude: Located approximately between 31° 20' and 37° N and 103° and 109° W.

Highest/lowest elevation: Wheeler Peak in Taos County, 13,161 feet (4,011 m)/Red Bluff Reservoir in Eddy County, 2,842 feet (866 m)

Hottest/coldest temperature: 122°F (50°C) on June 27, 1994 at Waste Isolation Pilot Plant/–50°F (–45.5°C) on February 1, 1951 at Gavilan

Land area/rank: 121,364 square miles (314,331 sq km)/5th

Inland water area: 234 square miles (606 sq km)

Population (2000 census)/rank: 1,819,046/36th

Population of major cities:

    Albuquerque: 448,607

    Las Cruces: 74,267

    Santa Fe: 62,203

    Roswell: 45,293

    Rio Rancho: 51,765

Origin of state name: Named after the country of Mexico by the first Spanish settlers in the region

State capital: Santa Fe (established 1610)

Previous capitals: San Juan de los Caballeros (established 1598), San Gabriel del Yunque (established 1600)

Counties: 33

State government: 70 representatives, 42 senators

Major rivers/lakes: Canadian River, Gila River, Pecos River, Rio Chama River, Rio Grande, San Juan River/Abiquiu Lake, Lake Avalon, Blue Hole, Bluewater Lake, Bottomless Lakes, Brantley Lake, Caballo Reservoir, Cochiti Lake, Conchas Reservoir, Eagle Nest, Elephant Butte Reservoir, El Vado, Heron Lake, Lake McMillan, Navajo Lake, Santa Rosa Lake, Storrie Lake, Sumner Lake, Ute Lake

Farm products: Alfalfa, apples, barley, cantaloupes, chiles, corn, cotton, grapes, hay, lettuce, milk, oats, onions, potatoes, peanuts, pecans, pinto beans, sorghum grain, sweet potatoes, tomatoes, wheat

Livestock: Beef cattle, hogs, chickens, sheep

Manufactured products: Aircraft parts, chemicals,

clothing, electrical and transportation equipment, electronics and computer products, lumber, machinery, plastics, petroleum and coal products, printing and publishing, processed food

Mining products: Bark, cedar, coal, clays, copper, firewood, gold, gypsum, helium gas, iron, lead, mesquite, natural gas, paper and pulp, petroleum, potash, pumice, sand and gravel, salt, silver, stone, uranium salts, wood chips, zinc

Animal: Black bear (*Oso negro*), adopted 1963

Bird: Chaparral or "roadrunner" (*Geococcyx californianus*), adopted 1949

Colors: Red and yellow, adopted 1925

Cookie: Biscochito, adopted 1989

Fish: Rio Grande Cutthroat Trout (*Onchorhynchus clarki virginalis)*, adopted 1955

Flower: Yucca (*Yucca glauca)*, adopted 1927

Fossil: Coelophysis (pronounced "see-LA-fisis"). An extinct warm-blooded carnivore weighing about 50 lbs (22.7 kg) and measuring about 6 ft (1.82 m); adopted 1981

Gem: Turquoise, adopted 1967

Grass: Blue grama (*bouteloua gracilis)*, adopted 1989

Insect: Tarantula hawk wasp, adopted 1989

Motto: *Crescit Eundo* (It Grows As It Goes)

Nickname: Land of Enchantment

Poem: "A Nuevo Mexico," adopted 1991

Question: "Red or green?" (referring to chiles—the question most often asked of diners when ordering traditional New Mexican cuisine), adopted 1996

Songs: "O, Fair New Mexico" (by Elizabeth Garrett), adopted 1917; "Así es Nuevo Méjico" (by Amadeo Lucero), adopted 1971

Tree: Piñon Pine *(Pinus edulis)*, adopted 1949

Vegetables: Chile and frijoles (pinto beans), adopted 1965

Wildlife: Barking frog, coral snake, collared and tree lizards, Couch's spadefoot toad, massassagua rattlesnake, narrowhead garter snake, yellow mud turtle, ducks, finches, Gambel's quail, geese, dusky grouse, great blue heron, hummingbirds, whooping crane (endangered), jays, lesser prairie chicken, pyrrhuloxia, raptors (including the golden eagle), greater roadrunner, greater and lesser sandhill cranes, swifts, thrashers, thrushes, wild turkey, vireos, warblers, woodpeckers, wrens, badger, beaver, black bear, bobcat, chipmunk, coyote, elk, gray fox, jackrabbit, javelina, marten, mink, mountain lion, mule deer, muskrat, otter, porcupine, prairie dog, pronghorn, raccoon, Rocky Mountain bighorn sheep, desert bighorn sheep (endangered)

TIMELINE

NEW MEXICO STATE HISTORY

1598 — Juan de Oñate founds the first Spanish capital, San Gabriel del Yunque

1610 — Spanish governor Pedro de Peralta founds a new capital, La Villa Real de Santa Fe de San Francisco de Asis (the Royal City of the Holy Faith of St. Francis of Assisi). Name is later shortened to Santa Fe

1680 — First Pueblo Revolt drives Spanish settlers out of Santa Fe

1696 — Second Pueblo Revolt breaks out

1821 — Mexico declares independence from Spain; Santa Fe Trail is founded

1850 — New Mexico becomes a U.S. territory

1864–1867 — Navajos and Apaches are forced to relocate to Bosque Redondo on the Long Walk

1879 — Railroad opens in New Mexico

1607 — The first permanent British settlement at Jamestown, Virginia

1620 — Pilgrims set up Plymouth colony

1776 — American colonies declare independence from England

1783 — American Revolutionary War ends

1787 — U.S. Constitution is written

1812–15 — U.S. and England fight the War of 1812

1843 — Pioneers travel West on the Oregon Trail

1846–48 — U.S. fights war with Mexico

1861–65 — Civil War occurs in the United States

UNITED STATES HISTORY

Reies Tijerina tries to seize government-owned land and return it to Hispanics; he takes two hostages, and is later arrested

Statewide drought causes major forest fires

World's first atomic bomb is exploded at Trinity Site near Alamogordo

Wildfire causes the evacuation of 25,000 people from Los Alamos and threatens the Los Alamos National Laboratory

Space shuttle *Columbia* lands at White Sands Missile Range

New Mexico becomes forty-seventh state

Rumors of a crashed UFO in Roswell make national headlines

1912   **1945** **1947**   **1967**   **1982**   **1996** **2000**

1917–18 **1929**   **1941–45**   **1950–53** **1964** **1965–73** **1969**   **1991** **1995**

U.S. takes part in World War I

Civil rights laws passed in the U.S.

U.S. and other nations fight in Persian Gulf War

U.S. fights in World War II

U.S. fights in the Vietnam War

The stock market crashes and U.S. enters the Great Depression

U.S. fights in the Korean War

Neil Armstrong and Edwin Aldrin land on the moon

U.S. space shuttle docks with Russian space station

GALLERY OF FAMOUS NEW MEXICANS

Ben Abruzzo and Maxie Anderson
(1930–1985) (1934–1983)
American balloonists who were first to cross the Pacific Ocean in the *Double Eagle V* in 1981. Anderson was also first to cross the Atlantic Ocean in a balloon in 1978. Both men lived in Albuquerque.

John Denver
(1943–1997)
Singer and songwriter who earned fame with songs such as "Leaving on a Jet Plane," "Take Me Home," and "Rocky Mountain High." Born in Roswell.

Alan Hale
(1958–)
Astronomer. One of two people who discovered the Hale-Bopp comet in 1995. Lived in Alamogordo.

Peter Hurd
(1904–1984)
American painter best known for his landscapes of New Mexico. He also painted a portrait of President Lyndon B. Johnson, which hangs in the Smithsonian's National Portrait Gallery in Washington, D. C. Born in Roswell.

John Nichols
(1940–)
Author and essay writer. His most famous novel is *The Milagro Beanfield War,* the first of three books about the people of New Mexico. It was made into a movie that was filmed in Truchas by actor and director Robert Redford. Lives in Taos.

Katherine D. Ortega
(1934–)
Served as 38th treasurer of the United States—the first Hispanic treasurer in U.S. history—from 1983 to 1989. She also served as an alternate representative to the United Nations General Assembly from 1990–1991. Born in New Mexico.

Eliot Porter
(1901–1990)
One of the first major photographers to work almost entirely with color film. Porter is best known for his nature photography. Lived in Santa Fe.

Bobby Unser and Al Unser
(1934–) (1939–)
National auto-racing champions. Together the brothers won seven Indianapolis 500 races (Al, shown right, won four; Bobby won three). Both men were born in Albuquerque.

GLOSSARY

adobe: brick or building material made of sun-dried earth and straw

arroyo: the bed of a creek or small stream that is usually dry

conquistador: Spanish word meaning "conqueror"; a term used to describe the leaders of the Spanish conquest of America and Mexico in the 1500s

controversy: an argument or dispute that goes on for a long period of time

drought: long period of dry weather

extinct: no longer in existence

humidity: moisture in the air; dampness

irrigate: to supply land with water through artificial means (i.e. spraying, flooding, etc.)

juncture: a place where two or more things meet

mesa: a high, steep-sided rock plateau

petroglyph: a prehistoric rock carving

precipitation: moisture that falls from the sky, such as rain, snow, or hail

pueblo: a large, multiroom dwelling made of adobe or stone built by Native Americans of the American Southwest; a town or village inhabited by Native Americans of the Southwest

scarce: available in a very limited amount

semi-arid: describes regions that get small amounts of rainfall, between 10 and 20 inches (25 and 51 cm) per year

yucca: state flower of New Mexico; a member of the lily family

FOR MORE INFORMATION

Web sites

All About New Mexico
http://www-psych.nmsu.edu/~linda/chilepg.htm
Hundreds of links relating to New Mexico's activities, attractions, foods, government, libraries, schools, and more.

From the Mountains to the Sea: A Slide Show of the Rio Grande
http://education.lanl.gov/resources/team/slideshow.html
A Flight Over the Rio Grande
http://education.lanl.gov/resources/team/flight.html
These sites provide beautiful photos of New Mexico's geographical features.

Gallup, New Mexico
http://www.gallupnm.org
Find out more about the largest Native American center in the Southwest.

New Mexico Department of Tourism
http://www.newmexico.org
Official web site of the New Mexico Department of Tourism; includes information about the state's cities, scenic attractions, history, and more.

Books

Meyer, Carolyn. *Río Grande Stories.* San Diego, California: Harcourt Brace, 1994.

Webb, David. *Adventures with the Santa Fe Trail: An Activity Book for Kids and Teachers* (revised edition). Dodge City, Kansas: Kansas Heritage Center, 1993.

Yoder, Walter D. *The Camino Real (the King's Road) Activity Book: Spanish Settlers in the Southwest.* Santa Fe, New Mexico: Sunstone Press, 1994.

Addresses

Albuquerque Convention & Visitors' Bureau
20 First Plaza, Suite 601
P.O. Box 26866
Albuquerque, NM 87125-6866

Pecos National Historical Park
P.O. Drawer 418
Pecos, NM 87552

Petroglyph National Monument
6001 Unser Boulevard, NW
Albuquerque, NM 87120

Santa Fe Convention & Visitors' Bureau
P.O. Box 909
Santa Fe, NM 87504-0909

INDEX

ABOUT THE AUTHOR

Therese De Angelis is an editor and the author of several children's books, including a biography of Jodie Foster, a book about the dangers of drug use, and an account of the 1979 accident at Pennsylvania's Three Mile Island nuclear power plant. She first became interested in New Mexico while writing a history about Native Americans and Spanish explorers. Ms. De Angelis lives in a suburb of Philadelphia, Pennsylvania, with a collection of pet birds.